This book may be kept

FOURTEEN DAYS

A fine will be charged for each day the book is kept overtime.

MR 9 '67			
AP 13 '67			
29.17 AP			
MY 18 '67			
NO 20			
GAYLORD 142			PRINTED IN U.S.A.

HAVE ONE ON ME

BY

Georgie Starbuck Galbraith

WITH DRAWINGS BY VAHAN SHIRVANIAN

J. B. Lippincott Company
PHILADELPHIA & NEW YORK

To all my editors, past and present, whose advice, criticism, praise and friendship have helped to keep the rewarding experience of writing from degenerating into a job.

ACKNOWLEDGMENTS

The author is indebted to the following publications in which certain of these poems first appeared:

Adam Bedside Reader, The American Home, The Atlantic Monthly, Ballyhoo (Dell Publishing Company, for "Wail at a Cocktail Party"), *Better Homes & Gardens, Chatelaine, The Christian Home, Cosmopolitan, D.A.C. News* (for poems on pages 23b, 27b, 44, 47, 66b, 97, 99, 104t, 111b), *The Diplomat Magazine* (for poems on pages 30t, 32b, 82, 115b, 123t, 124, 152, 154, 159), *Family Weekly* (for poems on pages 46, 48t, 53t, 55, 59, 64, 68), *Good Housekeeping, Hi Way, Ladies' Home Journal, McCall's, Maclean's, Management Review* (American Management Association, for "Prejudicewise"), *Quote* (for poems on pages 92b, 94b, 103m, 104m, 106m, 109b, 148–2; reprinted by permission), *New York Herald Tribune, The New York Times, The Saturday Evening Post, Saturday Night* (for poems on pages 83t, 106b, 107m, 153), *Saturday Review, The Wall Street Journal* (for poems on pages 18, 58, 92m, 96t, 108t, 119); *Woman's Life* and *Your Life*, permission Wilfred Funk.

Contents

HIS AND HERS

DOUBLE EXPOSURE

Contents

DOMESTIC DILEMMA

NOTHING TRIVIAL

AH, HOSPITALITY!

SERPENTS' TEETH

THE HAPPY APE

Contents

READER REACTION

PHILOSOPHY IS WHAT YOU MAKE IT

THE MAN IN THE AISLE SEAT

Contents

THE FACTS OF LOVE

A SEIZURE OF COUPLETS

SUMMARY

HAVE ONE ON ME

His and Hers

HIS AND HERS

It's a man's world? Perhaps it is,
But happily it occurs
That, though the planet is labeled HIS,
He is labeled HERS.

TRUTH OF THE MARTYR

She's given him, moans this martyred wife,
Some of the best years of her life.
And in addition, the plain truth is,
She's given him some of the worst of *his*.

DISTAFF DOUBLE

A man must ponder upon this pair
Of problems a woman has to face:
She has absolutely nothing to wear,
And she hasn't an inch of closet space!

THE PARIS DRESS

The girls are all pleased with her dress.
Its *couture* is the absolute *hautest*.
The neckline is cunning, the price tag is stunning.
The color is sure to be noticed.

And none of the girls has one like it,
For it's ages ahead of the minute.
So they eye it with pleasure, delighted past measure
To note she looks terrible in it.

TENSE SITUATION

You close your book and softly sigh
For gorgeous girls of days gone by,
And, "Helen!" breathe, and act as though
I were composed of dingy dough.
I know, my darling, what you wish.
I'll grant you Helen was a dish,
And Sheba probably could show me
Worse than up. I'll own Salome,
Cleopatra, and Susannah
Were sugar, spice, and grade-A manna.
But would you, dear, un-quo the status?
I wouldn't for the world free gratis.
For leave us not forget, my lad,
Those ladies' charms are charms they *had*,
While mine, though rather less immense,
Are active in the present tense.

THE ORDEAL AND TRIUMPH OF
LORELEI KLUMP

The glamour that captured and wholly enraptured
The husband of Lorelei Klump
Had frayed at the seams with the passing years.
She was, as she knew, a frump.

Well, loving her mate, she saw her duty:
She had to get back her verve and beauty.
So when her spouse took a business trip,
She leapt to the task and let 'er rip,
Embracing a regimen somewhat tougher
Than many accredited martyrs suffer:
She exercised till she dropped in her tracks;
She bore the masseuse's bruises and whacks.
Too tired to stand and too sore to sit,
She lived upon birdseed, coffee, and grit.

So by dint of courage and untold rigor,
She got back her glamour and girlish figger,
Which she was a-twitter to display
To her homing husband. So came the day:
Begirdled like Circe, her posture starched,
Her tresses re-styled and her eyebrows arched,
And—let's be honest—completely frazzled,
She welcomed her lord with a smile that dazzled.

And he took in his arms this bundle of charms,
Refurbished and twenty pounds thinner,
And beaming with pleasure, he spoke (I quote),
"Hi, sweetie pie. What's for dinner?"

SONG OF SOMEBODY'S HUSBAND

What need have I for gold? . . . when mine
Are all my darling's golden curls,
Her sapphire eyes that blaze and shine,
Her ruby lips, her teeth like pearls.

All rare and lovely wealth is she,
And for my miser heart enough.
What need have I for gold? Ah me,
My darling seems to eat the stuff!

MALE, FEMALE, AND MONEY, CREATED HE THEM

The argument is endless:
Men think that wives should spend less;
A thought wives couldn't spurn more.
They know that men should earn more.

NO SHOT AT SUNRISE

Many, my darling, the things I will do for you:
Sew on a button or buff up a shoe for you;
Trail you through galleries, jabbering artily;
Laugh at your stories both often and heartily.
Still, I would sooner retreat to a nunnery
Than to partake in your passion for gunnery;
Sooner give quarts of my loving heart's blood for you
Than to go scramble through bramble and mud for you,
Menacing bird-life while dawn squints a bleary eye
Over the landscape. My virilest dearie, I
Flatly exclude from the proofs of my love for you
One little pot-shot at one little dove for you!

THE PAT ON THE HEAD

From Sappho to Austen, from Sand to Millay,
All women of wit and sense
Have gritted their teeth and prickled beneath
That male-est of compliments.

Oh, none has eluded that pat on the head,
And none ever will or can:
Some knot-headed god will indulgently nod
And tell her she thinks like a man!

SAD TRUTH OF THE BACHELOR

Though loud his freedom's vaunted,
Remember, he's a chap
Whom so far no girl's wanted
Bad enough to trap.

LANGUAGE BARRIER

A wise man, easing domestic friction,
Soon learns to grapple with distaff diction,
And dig the rules of feminine jargon:
A worthless purchase is called a *bargain*;
Nothing to wear means nothing new;
Stew, when there's company, is *ragout*.
A man must grasp, once his good wife hints it,
That she doesn't dye her hair; she *tints* it;
Though he has an abdomen, she has a *tummy*;
What he'd call edible she terms *yummy*.

And mastery of the Femalese,
Whereby he interprets with practised ease
Remarks such as, "Dear, I *adore* Irene!
We're just not speaking, is all I mean,"
May well encourage a married man to
Pursue the simpler study of Bantu!

CROSS-QUESTION

Men, when their affairs require,
Must awhile themselves retire,
Sometimes hunt and sometimes hawk,
And not always sit and talk.
                    THOMAS CAMPION

Oh, tell me truly, Mr. C.,
Is that a sterling guarantee?
Can I be sure my noble squire
Eftsoons will to himself retire
And let me see to my affairs,
As per my charm and its repairs,
The laundry that I fain would launder,
And the quandaries I quandar?
Will he hunt and leave me time
In which to be the creature I'm
Besides a woman? . . . time to be a
Person nursing an idea
Quite her own, plus temper, moods,
Mosquito bites, and tastes in foods?
Oh, will he hawk, dear Mr. C.,
And give me time for being me,
A luxury that, with her lord,
A lady rarely can afford!

RETOUCHING STORY

Before a party, how doth milady?
For hours at her glass she squanders care
In seeing her eye shadow's not too shady,
Her lipstick's flawless, and so is her hair.

Perfection achieved, she gets in the car,
The windows hoisted the while she drives
A mile or so . . . it is never far.
And what doth milady when she arrives?

She heads for a mirror as cow to clover
To do her hair and her make-up over!

DINNER MOOD

Candle light guttering?
Masculine muttering:
Can't tell the bread
From the thumb he's buttering!

BALLADE OF THE HOMING HOUSE PETS

A man and a feline are apt to stray,
For cats and men are a restless crew.
They'll leave you to cope with the lonely day
And sniffle the silent midnight through,
While they make for a darkling rendezvous
Or hie to a secret bivouac.
But little's the profit to pursue.
Men and pussy-cats always come back.

Though you feed them on manna and speak them gay,
Never the man nor the tabby grew
Whose ear was deaf to the call to play.
Though their hearts be ever so staunch and true,
They're off with a blithesome toodle-oo
To the open road or the cul-de-sac.
Yet muster your patience for, *entre nous,*
Men and pussy-cats always come back.

Oh, cosset and coax them as ever you may,
Wheedle and worry and whistle and woo
And wait on their every whim, yet they
Will wander to Dallas or Timbuctu.
But la, why indulge in a hullabaloo
And shatter the family bric-a-brac?
With a "Hello, dear" and a plaintive mew,
Men and pussy-cats always come back.

L'Envoi
Princess, see that your sighs are few.
Ration your tears, for alas, alack,
Though you may not want them when they do,
Men and pussy-cats always come back!

Double Exposure

DOUBLE EXPOSURE

I gaze from my picture window,
And what is the view I see?
My neighbor's picture window
Getting a view of me,

Which gives me the same sensation
As I'd identify
With peeping through a keyhole
And looking at an eye.

SURE YOU REMEMBER HER, BEN BOLT!

Oh, don't you remember sweet Alice, Ben Bolt,
  Who at your smile broke down
And wept with delight, then trembled with fright
  Whenever you gave her a frown?
Well, I was just thinking what psychoanalysis
Could do for a bang-up case like Alice's!

SUBURBAN NOCTURNE

The Pruetts' Doberman barks and barks,
A captain of canine grouches.
Its yapping maddens the poor McFaddens,
Who rise from their rumpled couches
And turn on their TV good and loud.
This rouses the Browns' small moppet,
Whose angry howls awaken the Powells,
Who yell at the Browns to stop it.

The Browns switch all of their house lights on,
Including their shadeless porch light,
Which shines in the eyes of the neighboring Frys
With the glare of a well-trained torch light.
The Frys try phoning the Pruetts then
To offer some terse instruction
On quieting dogs, but the Pruetts are logs
Who sleep through the whole production!

WERE I A WITCH

Oh, I'd consign
To regions inky
People who pine
For a "little drinkie".

And I'd put a hex
On all those biddies
Of either sex
Who speak of "kiddies".

And were I a witch,
Be sure the blighters
I'd smite with itch
Are the "Nightie-Nighters"!

PRESS CLIPPING

Of many a public notable,
One fact is broadly hintable:
Those utterances most quotable
Are very rarely printable.

WHAT'S IN A MISNOMER?

When pigeonholes hold pigeons,
When dovetails grow on doves,
Then look in glove compartments
For gloves.

MODERN LIBERAL

He is a hot-eyed fellow who
Takes a most illiberal view
Of anyone whose viewpoint is
Not so liberal as his.

DEPARTMENT STORE DUCHESS

A *clerk?* This scion of dukes and princes,
Before whom my ego quails and winces?
My clothes turn ragged beneath her stare,
And I feel the prickle of hay in my hair.

She's left her tiara in the vault,
But she brushes me far below the salt
As five pearls drop at my swinish feet:
"May I help you, modom?" I can't retreat,
So I state my need. And with splendid languor
She shows me her treasures till, brave with anger,
I pay just twice what I can afford . . .
Which she meant I should. So I haven't scored.

No, still the lowest of lowly peasants,
I back away from the regal presence,
Pursued by an icy, "Thank you, modom,"
And wish I were God and she were Sodom!

SONG OF THE BUDGETEER

For housing and clothing, insurance and fun
Our needs are restrained by economy.
And no epicure's taste lays our budget in waste
With a passion for fancy gastronomy.

But it seems we're the victims of one appetite
As insatiable as it's spontaneous.
For monthly we buy an unholy supply
Of something that's called Miscellaneous!

FISCAL PHILOSOPHY

Ah, money! It is evil's root!
  Why crave it?
All wise men shun this long green loot
  And waive it.
For filthy lucre does no good.
And if that point's well understood,
I'll only add I wish I could
  Engrave it!

RHYME OF THE
GOOD LITTLE GIRL

By honest toil I earn my bread;
I'm modest as a sparrow.
There may be primrose paths to tread,
But mine's the straight and narrow.

A piece of flannel guards my chest
From wintry chills and quinsy.
I'm not the type to interest
The fans of Dr. Kinsey.

My soul is wholly free of debt,
And no one begs to buy it.
I've never seen an etching yet,
Nor tried a pottage diet.

My past is spotless all the way,
And just as pure and gleaming
The future waits. And some fine day
I'll scream and keep on screaming!

NO MIXED GREEN SALAD FOR ME, THANKS

I'll just take my greenery
In scenery.
I often speak harshly
Of parshley.
I won't make a fetish
Of lettish.
I'm disgustard with mustard
Esparshly.

Oh, hickory-chickory, into the discard!
Cabbage and water cress, spinach and Swiss chard:
These I bequeath to the Order *Rodentia,*
And emphasize loudly, beyond peradventia,

The jist of this trivia
I givia:
Food rife with chlorophyl
Is orophyl!

HEARTBREAK IN THE SUPERMARKET

The line to the checker was long and slow,
But I'm next at the checking stand, and oh,
I note with a shock that leaves me reeling
It's somebody else's cart I'm wheeling!

MOVIE CHARMER

Her beauty is such
It'd be unmatchable,
If only so much
Were not detachable!

INSTALLMENT BUYER'S BLUES

How bitter my cup!
How darkly I frown!
Each month I pay up
What I didn't pay down!

WEDDING GUEST

My dear, she's an absolute picture,
As lovely a bride as I've seen.
(And whoever sold her that dress should have told her
To buy a sixteen!)

And isn't the bridegroom a darling!
You'd look a long way and not match him.
He's handsome and brainy and charmingly zany.
(And how did she catch him!)

BLUE PRINT
FOR
RED TAPE

Socialism:
A system in which
You take all the money
Away from the rich
And spend it on bureaus
That plan to the cent
How the poor would get it
If it hadn't been spent.

TO AN ADVERTISEMENT WHICH URGES ME
TO "DARE TO BE NEW"

Dare to be new? This world, dear ad,
Abounds with people who dare like mad:
Who measure the vodka and blithely serve
Imported grasshoppers for hors d'ouevres;
Who sit cross-legged on the floor and gloat
At the highest hi-fi's highest note;
Whose neo-Freudian phobias burgeon
Thicker than caviar in a sturgeon.

We're both acquainted with people in swarms
Who dote on art in its abstract forms;
Who'd sell their molars like so much gravel
To finance a fling at lunar travel.
In fact, dear ad, there is such a crew
Of people today who dare to be new
That it takes real courage for anybody
To dare, like me, to be fuddy-duddy!

PREJUDICEWISE

Such terms as *taxwise*
And *jobwise* and *strikewise*
Inspire me axwise
Or gunwise. Likewise?

OFF THE RECORD

Waste not your curse
On the d.j.'s chatter.
You'll need it worse
When he plays the platter!

MOTORIST'S MADRIGAL

My heart leaps up when I behold
The guy who passed me at a stop
Parked meekly curb-side being told
The facts of traffic by a cop!

RHYME OF THE MODERN MARINER

It is the Modern Mariner,
And he cometh from afar
With his speedboat on its trailer rack
A-sway behind his car.

Alone, alone, all, all alone!
Alone on a wide, wide plain:
That's what the fellow seems to think
As he blocks the inside lane.

And woe betide the wedding guest
Or others who would pass.
He swerveth right, he swerveth left,
And treadeth on the gas.

He raceth down, he creepeth up.
If he's no better sailor
Than helmsman of the open road,
A-hauling boat and trailer,

Methinks mayhap tomorrow night,
As homeward he doth rocket,
He'll block no traffic with that boat.
There'll be no boat to block it!

SORT OF AN ODE TO SLEEP

O sleep, thou child of Morpheus,
I twang my lyre like Orpheus
And serenade you. You're a pet,
Although of late we've scarcely met.

For while I toss and kick the covers,
You favor far less worthy lovers,
Enjoying shameless midnight trysts
With tax evaders, Communists,
Reformers, critics, TV sponsors
And nudists and Parisian tonsors.

In short, O sleep, you're none too choosy.
So come, my poppy-laden floozy;
Accept my song and grant my plea:
Crawl in and spend the night with me!

Domestic Dilemma

DOMESTIC DILEMMA

Some people are natural pillow-plumpers
And raveling gleaners and ash tray-dumpers.
And some are as natural pillow-wrinklers
And carpet-trackers and ashes-sprinklers.

And sooner shall feathers grow on rabbits
Than either will stoop to the other's habits,
Which makes the home life of both types brambly,
There being one each in every fambly!

THE LEFT-OVER PROBLEM

It's a little too little to save
And a little too much to dump
And nothing to do but eat it
That makes the housewife plump!

RHYME COMPOSED WHILE SLAVING OVER
A HOT CAN OPENER

What shall I cook? Ah, that is the question!
What *I* like bothers his indigestion;
What *he* likes makes my allergies strike;
And we're fed up with what both of us like!

DEN FATHER

In modern homes a den is the place
   Where a man can be alone
With a radio, a TV set,
A sewing machine, a bassinet,
An ironing board, some drying sweaters,
A stack of bills and unanswered letters,
   And three kids using the phone!

PERFECT MATCH

Now, Frederic Trent was a bachelor gent
Whose house was a one-man establishment.
His dishes, unwashed, ranged in columns and tiers.
He hadn't defrosted the reefer in years.
The papers lay scattered from numerous Sundays,
And thumb tacks and bailing wire fastened his undies.
One saw at a glance that Fred's dwelling was much
In need of what's known as the feminine touch.

A girl with no spouse was Miss Susie Bell Krauss,
Who lived all alone in an over-sized house
Where the water-taps sniffled, and one of her chairs
Was shakily pleading for vital repairs.
The clothes lines were sagging, a drain wouldn't drain,
And even a cursory glance made it plain
That Susie Bell's dwelling was much in demand
Of what is described as a masculine hand.

Then Susie met Freddie, or Freddie met Sue,
And the upshot was love, as they ardently knew.
They married and live in connubial bliss,
And a glance at their manse shows you something like this:
The dishes aren't washed nor the reefer defrosted;
The buttons from all of Fred's undies are losted;
The clothes lines are sagging; that rickety chair . . .
Go on, gentle reader, you take it from there!

SITTING PRETTY

I'll stick to my chair barring flood or fire.
I'll stick to my chair like a tack to a tire.
For once on my feet, I know what I'll hear:
"Mother dear . . .
As long as you're up, will you bring me a drink?"
"As long as you're up, will you fetch some ink?"
"As long as you're up, could you get me a sweater?"
"As long as you're up, wind the clock, you better."
"Will you let out the cat? Will you call the pup?"
"Will you close the window as long as you're up?"
So I'll stick to my chair and I'll keep sitting
Till somebody's up and can hand me my knitting.

GETTING-READY RHYME

Sing a song of swivets!
Papa's in the shower.
He'll hog the steamy sanctum
At least another hour.

Baby's dressed and waiting,
And what on earth's she doing,
So quiet in the kitchen?
Opening the bluing.

Junior's in the basement
Accumulating dirt,
And sister's in the bedroom
Wailing, fix her skirt!

So guess who's in a tizzy,
And steady, woman, steady,
When set to go, they chorus,
"Gee, Mom, aren't you *ready!*"

CANTICLE OF THE PANTRY

Bereft of storage,
We four-by-fourage;
Of any victual
Lay in but lictual.
For with celluloid collars
And $1.00 dollars
And Elmer Gantry,
We buried the pantry.

Old-fashioned pantries!
They may have been antries
And mouse reservations,
But they held rations.

Yes, along with roasters
And marshmallow toasters
And lost red mittens
And cats with kittens
And crocks and aluminum,
They still had ruminum
For—joy incredible!—
All things edible.

I grant they were clumsy,
But take it from Mumsy,
For all their gaucheries,
They held graucheries!

HOT WORDS
WITH A COLD
SUPPER

Ah yes, dear spouse,
I've been cleaning house
Till I've got more flop
Than a worn-out mop.
So unless you vote
For a *table d'hote*,
Stop biting the hand which
Feeds you the sandwich!

THE YOLK'S ON ME

Eggs à la Suisse? Or Eggs Mornay?
I leap to my stove to tackle
The fanciest dish of eggs you could wish
As quick as a hen could cackle.

Nor matters how tricky the recipe
On which I have gaily gambled;
Les Oeufs au Crème or les Oeufs Suprême
Will come out la même: Oeufs Scrambled!

WEEK-END QUESTIONNAIRE

1) Who'll take this stack of reports home to check over the week-end?

The boss came in too fast to duck:
Our hero's stuck.

2) Who'll drive Brownie Troupe 5 to Lake Ickypoo Saturday afternoon for the cook-out contest?

His youngest pipes up loud and shrill,
"My daddy will!"

3) Who'll go down to the church a couple of hours early Sunday morning and start the furnace?

For this slight task his wife enrolled him,
And then she told him.

4) Where can the Dillydown Little Theater Players hold a rehearsal Sunday evening?

His daughter's pear-shaped tones we catch:
"Chez moi, but natch!"

5) Who is that fellow muttering in his beer at the end of the tavern bar?

His face, though worn, unshorn, and chillier,
Is sure familiar!

EASY DOES IT . . . OR DOES IT?

Housekeeping is, say many men,
A snap. There's nothing to it.
They mean, of course, housekeeping when
Some woman's there to do it.

HOME-OWNER'S LAMENT

By the time it's paid for
From attic to basement,
Everything in it
Needs replacement!

A LONG LIFE AND A MERRY ONE

Oh, women live longer than men,
So clearly it's up to a wife
To shield her protector, then,
From the stress of domestic life.

She must send her lord to the daily grind
Armored with shining peace of mind,
And cope with the cares that her day may hold,
Viz., Junior seems to be taking a cold,
And the baby's raising an awful fuss . . .
Get going, you kids, or you'll miss the bus! . . .
And the plumbing clogs, and the washer quits
After tearing a brand-new sheet to bits,
And the door-bell shrills and the telephone shrieks,
And it starts to rain and the back porch leaks,
And the kids come home and behave like weasels,
And Junior's cold's not a cold, it's measles . . .

Yes, women live longer than men,
Or that's what the experts say.
And women can tell you when
It certainly seems that way!

Nothing Trivial

NOTHING TRIVIAL

Who has a cold none's meaner than?
A man.
Who'll treat this illness as a trifle?
His wife'll.
What colds arouse her real concern?
Hern.

POSTSCRIPT TO A
NO VISITORS SIGN

This placard wouldn't be posted
If it weren't essential to stem
The steady stream of people
Who think it doesn't mean *them!*

VALID MALADY

You're nursing a pain or visceral static?
She gives you the proof that it's psychosomatic.
She's well-informed, for she's read a book,
And quotes you the sacred gobbledegook:
Repression, compulsion, escapist device.
She diagnoses you in a trice,
And whether duodenal or dental,
The roots of your trouble are plainly mental.

So when she's ill, she takes to her bed,
And never a needless word is said
Of psychosomatics. For boy, oh boy,
When *she* gets sick, it's the real McCoy!

THE VENGEANCE OF CREEPINGTON BROWN

Creepington Brown was a people-hater,
A misanthrope unadorned.
And he sought for a means of venting his spleen
On the fellow men he scorned.

He dreamed of inflicting a combination
Of sheer discomfort, humiliation,
And impotent fury; some outrage which
He could visit alike on poor and rich.
And what he conceived was a piece of clothing
The entire race would regard with loathing:
A vesture no human alive could fit in,
Too short to stand in, much less to sit in,
Exposing the rear of the stuffiest vicar
Or merchant prince to a vulgar snicker,
And making a clown of a duke or banker.
Creepington chuckled with merry rancor.

Yes, this was the way to get even with people,
Thought creepy Creepington Brown.
So the dirty varmint invented the garment,
And called it the Hospital Gown!

THE HUMAN MALE
or
Achilles' Heel Isn't Weak until He
Gets a Blister on It

The human male will doggedly sail
Through treacherous ice-blocked seas
To map the snow on some polar floe
While his months'-long whiskers freeze.
Or fighting jungles, he'll bravely track
Ferocious beasts to their lair,
To snare 'em and truss 'em and bring 'em back,
Intrepid and debonaire.

Yes, scorning hardships and laughing at peril,
His spine as straight as his rifle barrel,
He studies voodoo and tribal rites,
Or charms a cobra before it bites,
And manages feats of derring-do
That simply amaze me through and through.

For this hero hale is the selfsame male
Who, when he bides at home,
Lies limp on his couch, a quivering grouch,
With a little cold in his dome;
Who plucks at the coverlid, weak and wan,
When threatened by tonsillitis,
Or moans like a saint with his thumbscrews on
At the least hint of neuritis.

So whenever I read of how dauntless men
Are planning magnificent deeds again,
Like scaling some new Tibetan mount
Through rigors and dangers beyond all count,
I always pray that they'll make it minus
The black defeat of a touch of sinus!

❧ RELAPSE

or

Roses are red and cactus is prickly;
Get out of that bed and stop acting sickly!

or

Hi-diddle-diddle, we hope the old kid'll
Soon be healthy and fit as a fiddle!

Oh, quick call the doctors and nurses!
I'm sinking! I'm sunk! I feel rotten!
I just finished reading the verses
On all those Get-Well cards I've gotten!

HOSPITAL HOSPITALITY

They've flung the NO VISITORS sign away.
You're convalescent, and so today
Your friends and kith will be in to spread
Bright rays of cheer round your hospital bed.

And they come in coveys, their greetings hearty.
Your room soon sounds like a cocktail party.
There's Tim telling jokes to Beth and Sue.
You can't hear the stories, for Jack and Lew
Are drowning them out with yak about golf.
So somebody carries your ashtray off,
And your water tumbler soon follows after,
Which nobody notes, with the talk and laughter.

For cheer is spread like a tax-payer's gold,
Though a medicine dropper wouldn't hold
What's aimed at the bed and the wallflower in it,
Who's feeling seedier by the minute!

CANTO IN A CLINIC

They test your blood by pints and quarts.
They fill you up with barium
And watch your blushing innards flip
Like fish in an aquarium.

They puncture you like needle-point.
They steal your clothes and drag you
From whatiscope to whosiscope.
They pummel, thump, and gag you.

For there's a test for every ill
To help the doctor cure it.
But few except the well and strong
Are able to endure it!

Ah, Hospitality!

AH, HOSPITALITY!

How sweet to greet the welcome guest
And give him sustenance and rest;
To sit with him for half the night
In confab serious or light;
Then tuck him in your own soft bed
And on the sofa lay your head.

And in the morning, sweet indeed
To yield the bathroom to his need,
Then break his fast with royal food.
Ah, hospitality! How good!
What else, mine host, so warms the heart,
Except to see the guest depart!

WHY HOSTESSES LEAVE HOME

Though the late dinner guest is a sinner
I'd like to see socially spurned
As the cause of an overcooked dinner
And a hostess as thoroughly burned,
I'll pardon the villain far liefer
Than the guest who arrives at an hour
While the food is still raw in the reefer,
The hostess the same in the shower!

TO A TOO, TOO GRACIOUS HOSTESS

Dear lady, by all means, tact; yet bear
One thought, come weal, come woe:
Tact is society's underwear;
It's not supposed to show.

BOHEMIAN CLAM BAKE

Each neo-Bohemian strikes a pose,
And the Intellectuals babble.
The Artist for Art's sake looks down his nose
At the money-grubbing rabble.

So it's hey for the vodka! Ho for the gin,
As the smoke and the tongues grow thicker!
And woe to the Babbitt who wanders in,
Unless he's providing the likker.

For Freedom is what they're enamored of:
An ardent passion foreboding
A staunch support of free verse, free love,
And especially free loading!

POTLUCK

For three days past their strength has been taxed,
And the entire house has been scrubbed and waxed.
For they're having the Smithers over to dine.
They've laid in candles and quaint little wine.
She's borrowed the ice cream forks from Mabel,
And cut-work place mats gladden the table.
She's whipped up a sumptuous repast.
And the Smithers are here at last, at last!

And limp as a squid from the three-day hassel
Now sits milord in his gleaming castle,
Amazed at hearing his helpmeet bubble,
"But we didn't go to the slightest trouble!
(Darling, go fetch the caviar.)
You'll just have to take us the way we are!"

WAIL AT A COCKTAIL PARTY

This bore babbles on with might and main,
And if rescue fails, alas,
They'll find me here in the corner slain
By the jawbone of an ass!

SIMPLE SELF DEFENSE

An hour at a cocktail party makes
    One general law declarable:
Some hoist their grog like accomplished rakes;
    In fact, their behavior's terrible.
But most guests drink no more than it takes
    To make the first group bearable.

THE TIDY GUEST

A neater guest was never seen.
He always keeps the ash trays clean
By smudging cigarettes in places
Like wash bowls, coffee cups, and vases.

DAWN PATROL

The quieter guests long since have departed.
But what of the antic, the merry-hearted?
Their get-up-and-go has given way
To a dogged spirit of sit-down-and-stay!

LINES COMPOSED
WHILE TRYING TO MAKE OUT
A GUEST LIST FOR A DINNER PARTY

I'm a person of no little erudition:
I know why the porcupine's spiny;
Why horses sleep in a standing position,
And why the planets are shiny.

I know why the hump's on the dromedary,
And why a chicken eats gravel.
But why people marry the people they marry
Is something I'll never unravel!

LINES COMPOSED WHILE
EMPTYING FORTY-SEVEN
ASH TRAYS

Oh, I love a party! . . . The guests so gay,
And the drinks passed round on a silver tray,
Including the number I'll later wince
To find got spilled on the floor and chintz;
The buffet supper, with candles gleaming,
The ham sliced thin, and the lobster steaming,
The charlotte russe that is so delicious,
And hundreds and hundreds of dirty dishes!

Oh, I love a party, with quips and laughter,
But I'll confess on the morning after
I love it better if it was thrown
In anyone's house except my own!

OFF MY LIST

The lovelorn swain returneth to the maid;
The swallow cometh back to Capistrano,
But never to this house the jerk who laid
A lighted cigarette on my piano!

SPARTAN PROLOGUE

The Cubs are off to have a cook-out.
They're going up to old Mt. Look-Out
To scorch their meat on open fires
As burnt as any child desires,
Acquiring, by such rustic rigors,
Strong characters and scores of chiggers,
So that in years to come they'll go
To dinner in a patio
And cope with steaks both charred and raw,
And fight the smoke that serves to draw
The bugs from miles around, in sooth.
The cook-outs of their early youth
Will turn the Cubs to men of strength
Who'll fill their country's breadth and length
With gallant heroes tough enough
For gracious living in the rough!

Serpents' Teeth

SERPENTS' TEETH

You're dedicated to parenthood:
You rear your offspring the way you should.
You tend their needs with a saint's endurance,
And take out a lot more life insurance.
You wipe their noses and bind up their bruises,
You nurse their mumps and provide 'em with shoeses
And dental braces that leave you pelfless.
You're in there pitching, dead-beat and selfless
And asking for more. For nobody ever
Had kids so adorable, cute, and clever.

And that "*Whoosh!*" you hear is the passing years.
And meanwhile, what of those cherub dears
For whom your hopes are as high as a steeple?
The little ingrates grow into *people!*

WHAT ARE BABIES MADE OUT OF?

The first one's made out of pink meringue
That wouldn't withstand a bump or bang:
Its parents believe it will break at a touch.
The second one's fragile, but not so much.
It's made out of something like well-baked cake.
The third is the one that will not break,
And parents relax and joyfully pounce
On a rubber baby that they can bounce.

THE MUD PIE SET

Oh, if there's a coal bin,
The small fry will crawl in it.
If there's a puddle,
Be sure they will sprawl in it.
Blithely intent on
Consuming their pound of dirt,
Life for the moppets
Is one giddy round of dirt.
Squirting what's squirtable,
Squashing what's squashable,
Children, thank heaven,
Are guaranteed washable!

ADVANCED PSYCHOLOGY

"The toddler is an egocentric who
understands things only in terms
of what he does with them: *a
hole is to dig*."
                    CHILD PSYCHOLOGIST

Ah, egocentric tot,
As guileless as your dimple,
How happy is your lot,
To think a hole's so simple.

Dig while you can, sweet youth.
Too soon will you begin to
Discern this deeper truth:
A hole's for falling into!

FROM THE EIGHT-YEAR-OLD'S
DICTIONARY

Wells are to holler down;
Cracks, to lose a dollar down.
Cellars are to hide down;
Banisters, to slide down.
Chairs are to wriggle in;
Church is to giggle in.
Lessons are to fuddle you,
And grandmas, to cuddle you.

Puddles are to splash through;
Flower-beds, to dash through;
Heads, to balance plates on;
Stairs, for leaving skates on.
Doors are for slamming;
Pockets are for cramming,
And parents are to shove you
And coax and scold and love you.

PARENTAL CONJECTURE
AT A DOUBLE-FEATURE

Junior is chopping the table
With his trusty little axe.
Sister is strewing the bathroom
With pretty carpet tacks.

The baby just tangled with Rover
And Rover was badly bitten.
And where is the baby sitter?
Sittin'!

GENUS AMERICANUS

Pedestrians are
Those folks with one
Family car
And teen-age son.

AS PREDICTED

Now, Percival Watt as a child was a model:
A minion of duty, but no mollycoddle.
He laundered his ears and he brushed every tooth;
He lapped up his carrots, and told only truth.
His piggy bank bulged as his pennies accrued;
He practised his oboe, and never was rude.
And everyone said that if ever a tot
Was marked for big things, it was Percival Watt.

But Johnny McCoy was a different type:
He feasted on apples before they were ripe;
He fibbed, and he squandered his pennies like water,
And often said things that no gentleman oughter.
He socked little girls; and in order to drag him
To bed it was helpful to bind him and gag him.
And people averred that if ever a boy
Was headed for grief, it was Johnny McCoy.

Well, Percival Watt proves how right people are:
He grew up to be an industrial czar,
A clubman and deacon. And people say, "See,
We knew from the start that is what he would be."
And Johnny McCoy, what of that little goon?
He grew up, like Percy, to be a tycoon,
A clubman and deacon. And people say, "Yes,
We knew from the start he would be a success."

75

INSCRIPTION
FOR A
HAIRBRUSH

Believe in spanking I do not,
Yet spank with this apology:
My child believes still less, God wot,
In modern child psychology!

MIDAS OF THE LAWN MOWER

Our stripling lad's in clover now.
A plutocrat, he labors
With sweat upon his earnest brow,
A-gardening for the neighbors.

So beautifully their yards are kept,
They handsomely reward him.
I'd hire the kid myself except
I simply can't afford him!

THREE PHASES OF EVE

Our tomboy scorns the sight of soap,
Although I plead and scold.
But I hang on and cope and hope.
It's just a phase, I'm told.

Her sister's married to the phone,
From which she never stirs.
In vain I reason, moan, and groan.
It's just a phase of hers.

And if I climb the walls some days,
I hope it's understood
I'm merely passing through a phase.
They call it "motherhood"!

SERIOUS LITTLE TALK

That's when a parent, with stammering tongue
And many a blush, engages
In explaining to his innocent young
What the kids have known for ages.

TEEN-AGE TRAGEDY

If he finds her dad in his ancient slippers,
This godling who is her date,
Or the house hints hauntingly of kippers,
She weeps for Creation's fate.

The sun will freeze and the moon will shatter
And shame will curdle the sea.
For youth is when things that do not matter
Matter terribly.

YOUNG DOG, OLD TRICKS

One glance at our stripling's anguished face
Is all we need to tell us
His girl is leading a merry chase,
And he is greenly jealous.

Hourly he phones his captious dear,
His pride reduced to pleading.
Why they call it "puppy love" is clear,
For a dog's life's what he's leading!

OLD FALLACY

A small forsaken ghost, she trails
About the house and bites her nails
And stares through space with stricken eyes.
She mopes and fidgets, frets and sighs,
And fights the tears that would betoken
A vernal heart quite newly broken.
And this is pain as sharp and sure
As any human hearts endure.
And this is sorrow that might chill
Souls far more seasoned to such ill.

Heigh-ho, the carefree days of youth!
Whoever first so quoth, forsooth,
He had a loose and lying tongue,
Or else the knave was never young!

COUNT-DOWN

The chore of launching a lunar rocket
(Yes, dear, you may borrow my sapphire locket)
Can scarcely entail more toil and care
(You certainly *may not* bleach your hair!)
And strain on the higher echelon
(I told you, baby, the straps stay *on!*)
Nor sharper checking of weather maps
(It won't rain, pet . . . and I said, *with straps!*) . . .

I was saying: launching a lunar shot
(Use make-up, dear; it's a little spot)
Can't be more wearing on grit and gristle
Than biding the hour when our guided miss'll
Go out of this world in a soaring flight
To her first big formal dance tonight!

The Happy Ape

THE HAPPY APE

The happy ape, he does not weep.
Content with food, a place to sleep,
A mate or two, his jungle heath,
The sky above, the earth beneath,
He does not buy, he does not sell.
He wots no sin, invents no hell,
Does homage to no suzerain,
And makes no war for god or gain.

Nor clock nor creed can call him slave.
He does not toil nor spin nor shave.
He has no pants to harbor ants
In re finances or romance,
And needs no cocktails to escape
From fear or boredom. Happy ape!
Let someone prove, if prove he can,
The ape did not descend from man.

THE INSCRUTABLE CAT

She crouches, a silent golden sphinx,
And thinks and drowses and yawns and thinks . . .
Of cosmic riddles old as Osiris?
Behold her there like a fur-swathed heiress,
A jewel-eyed hedonist whose mind
Is filled with the thoughts of her occult kind:
Herself and her own desires. In short,
Will I let her stay on the davenport
Or put her out? And dare she try
To capture a goldfish by-and-by?
Veiled and inscrutable, she hunches
And ponders profoundly how soon lunch is.

THE VAGRANT

For shame, you jaded bee!
I watched you all the day:
From tavern unto tavern
You reeled your giddy way.

Now, ending your carouse,
Besotted you repose
Afar from hive and mother
Within a wine-flecked rose.

ON RESCUING
A JAY-WALKING TORTOISE
FROM AN ASPHALT GRAVE

Poor innocent bucolic reptile,
Out across the street you've crept till
Hissing lines of traffic hurtle
All about you. Trusting turtle!
For though old Aesop was aware
Of how the tortoise beat the hare,
Drivers doing fifty per
May not recall the fable, sir.
While slow but sure could be the pace
To best a bunny in a race,
When crossing any busy street,
Equip yourself with rabbit's feet!

TO A MOUSE

Though death will trap you in the end,
Could I, a fellow pilgrim, friend,
Be a smug party to your doom?
I know that you didn't ask to come
Into the perilous world you live in,
Where honest mice are often driven
To thievery by empty bellies.
You don't beg heaven for cakes and jellies,
But merely a little cheese and bread,
The chance of a roof above your head,
And the simple right to be a mouse.
So be it. You're welcome in this house,
And may the trifling boon suffice
To justify God's ways to mice.

THE MOLE TO ITS CHILD

My son, we burrow underground
Through cold and damp and dark.
The lot to which our race is bound
Is harsh indeed. Yet mark
That though we are by nature blind,
Yet heaven favors moles.
For of all creatures God designed,
Only the moles have souls.

WHAT'S A WATCH DOG?

A watch dog is a dog who's staunch
To nip on ankle, thigh, and haunch
Such brash intruders on his acres
As meter men or census takers
Or wealthy uncles come to call;
And then to lick the hand of all
Who peddle brush or greeting card;
And in the night, still standing guard,
With blissful wag and canine gurgle,
To welcome folk who come to burgle.

ADVICE TO A BIRD, SPECIES UNKNOWN

Listen to me, you silly bird,
Has no one told you? Haven't you heard
That the winters here are long and cold?
Then harken, bird: you are being told.
Be on your way! Go south! Get going!
Any time now it may be snowing . . .
Sleet and hail and a mean wind blowing.
Winter is here. Didn't you know that?
And winter's a crusty old gray cat . . .
Ice on his whiskers, frost on his paws.
He'll gobble you up in his freezing jaws!
He'll snap you up in his arctic mouth!
I'm telling you, bird, be bright. Go south!

ON HAVING MEANT WELL

My clumsy hand
Fumbles to catch the spider in the sink
And lift her out to dryer safer land.
But she, poor soul, must think
It's doom incarnate. Desperate and nimble,
She eludes my fingers in a dizzy chase in
The slippery basin,
Then . . . does her wild heart weigh the awful gamble? . . .
Leaps headlong down the drain
To drown, quite likely . . . while I stand and grumble
That all my good intentions were in vain.

BUTTERFLY

Immaculate as the scented air you ride,
Beautiful as the flower you deign to pilfer,
You drift and bask and preen in languid pride,
An exquisite in silken black and sulphur,

Foreign to struggle. Yet within your core
Still latent lies the gross barbarian.
Remember, Ariel, you lately wore
The crawling twisted shape of Caliban.

THE PHILOSOPHER

"My friend," I spake the Three-toed Sloth,
"Pray tell me why you are so loath
To leave your slothful ways?" He smiled,
"Why, I'm a philosopher, my child.
And action, it is my conclusion,
Is but a snare, a vain delusion.
The fullest life's in contemplation
Of life. My idle meditation
Is in the very best tradition;
So too my upside-down position.
Philosophers," the Sloth asserted,
"Have always viewed the world inverted."

WAKING WORLD

The east with rosy fingers
Shuts up the four-o'-clocks.
The morning star still lingers,
And golden crow the cocks.

Now dogs salute each other,
The hare hops from its hole,
And by its placid mother
Scampers the long-legged foal.

Up from the gilded steeple
The singing lark takes flight,
And myriad weary people
Awake and curse the light.

READER REACTION

Those novelists leave me completely unstirred
Who seem to believe that "psychology"
Is a synonym for a three-letter word
That's a synonym for "biology"!

ENCOMIUM COMPOSED IN A BOOK SHOP

Though many a novelist follows his star
To fame and the upper income brackets,
The masters of modern fiction are
Those dreamers who write the blurbs on the jackets!

HEAVY READING

A lot of historical novels, I've found,
Are apparently written to sell by the pound.

FROM BARD TO VERSE

Bards of Passion and of Mirth,
Had ye lived today on earth;
Had ye, Homer, Ovid, Horace,
This year raised your lilting chorus;
Had ye, Chaucer, Donne, and Byron,
Shaped your lays of fire and i-ron
In the present century,
I'd have never heard of ye.

These are times, believe me, Bards,
When a publisher regards
Poets as a fiscal bane.
Cookbooks sell; so does Spillane;
Even tomes on building muscles.
But, like buggy whips and bustles,
Poetry's outlived its day.
Rhyme, like reason, doesn't pay.

Bards, ye'd now be to the Trade
As pariahs. Ye would fade,
With the golden wealth ye minted,
Broke, unhonored, and unprinted!

REAL SWITCH

The basic plot of the murder thriller
I'd read with many a gladsome cry
Is one where a smart cop finds the killer
In spite of a stupid private eye.

NOVEL HANDICAP

Orientals are deemed unsuitable
For literature if they are scrutable.

TOP BANANA

This author has got it made;
No vestige of doubt now lurks.
For consider this accolade:
His books are known as Works.

SONNET SANS SEQUENCE

No female poet worthy of the name
Has failed in meeting prosody's great test:
To find and love a man . . . Oh, kingly best! . . .
Who roused her Muse to dip her quill in flame
And pen a sonnet sequence to proclaim
Her lord's rare virtues. Jewel-crowned and dressed
In purple walk these gods made manifest
In sonnets that have won their writers fame.

Alas, I sit and sigh with silent lyre!
For candidly, the gay old dogs and puplets
Whom I encounter with depressing frequence
Are not the sort of fellows to inspire
A lady poet to a brace of couplets,
Much less the labor of a sonnet sequence!

À PROPOS DE RIEN *

A pox on that show-off writer's pen,
Who renders his meaning murkish
By throwing in phrases I do not ken
In Latin or French or Turkish.

And a double pox if, grabbing a chance
For lingual ostentation,
The fellow insults my ignorance
By adding a coy translation!

*It's fixing to rain.

LOW-DOWN

I try to read 'em, but heaven bless me,
Elevating books depress me!

POETIC LICENSE EXPIRED

The writers of lyrics of popular songs
Are masters of lyrical language
Depicting love's ecstasies, longings, and wrongs,
And filling my heart with anguage.

Oh, it's not when they whimper of Swanee and Mammy
My blood runs cold and my hands go clammy.
No, it's when they feel this love can't be reel,
And cry for one kiss from their heart's ideel,
For by stars above and the moon on high,
This night of love is for you and I,
So darling, be kind to a lovesick fool!
Be tender, surrender, and don't be crool!
Be gentle! We'll rentle ittle home
Where life will be beautiful as a pome! . . .
Ah, then's when it seems that my dreams are filled
With mem'ries of having a molar drilled.

For the writers of lyrics of popular songs
Are the lads who will never extinguish
Love's passionate flame. But it's a shame
What they don't mind doing to Enguish!

97

WHODUNIT HEROINE

When the body in the study is discovered, knifed and bloody,
Does our heroine let loose and yell, "Police!"?
Don't be silly or absurder. She is sure they'd pin the murder
On herself, or it may be her little niece.

For the gendarmes are regarded as so mentally retarded
That they couldn't stalk a homicidal skunk.
So the corpse, in scenes dramatic, she lugs gamely to the attic
Where of course she hides it in the hero's trunk.

Then she tucks the murder weapon in the mattress that she's
    slep' on,
Wipes the fingerprints from every door and pillar,
Also burns important papers (it's a rule in all such capers),
Then she telephones . . . but not the cops, the killer.

So with all the clues well tangled, she gets nearly shot or
    strangled,
But she trusts and alibis the killer often,
So the stupid dicks are baffled, and the villain ain't yet snaffled
When they fit another victim with a coffin.

Now, in all this grim confusion I arrive at one conclusion:
If the cops are knuckleheads in murder shockers,
If they gibber like gorillas as they ferret out the killers,
It is heroines like ours who tipped their rockers!

THE JEJUNE JOURNALIST

There was a young reporter, so I've heard,
Who in his copy never once referred
To *holocausts*. He called them fires instead.
He didn't write *deceased* when he meant dead,
Nor *rap* for criticize, nor *filched* for stolen,
Nor did he call a senator a *solon*,
Nor *nab* law-breakers when they fled with *loot*.
No traveler by him was termed *en route*.
He never *probed*, *protested*, *flayed*, nor *balked*,
Nor said that people *parleyed* when they talked.
No *socialite* nor *scion* graced his copy,
And all in all, his writing was so sloppy
His editor was justly *irked* or *ired*,
And he was *sacked* . . . that's journalese for fired.

THE LOVESICK MUSE

I gather from authors' interviews
That most of them deal with a lovesick Muse
Who fawns and delivers the goods in reams.
For writing's a minor chore, it seems,
To mothers of six who blithely breed
Chinchillas and orchids, and read and read;
Or gents running ranches single-handed,
Who boast of the thousand steers they branded
While shoeing a horse and painting the barn
And hammering out that marvelous yarn.

Since authors are truthful as snow is black,
Oh, tell me what aphrodisiac
Or potion they slip in the Muse's drinks
That turns her into an amorous minx?
For here by the hour I've sweat, I've bled,
And what have I written? What you just read!

IN ONE GRAY CELL
AND OUT THE OTHER

What loving labors have I designed
Through hopeful years to improve my mind!
I've slogged through Tacitus, pondered the Persians,
Revered Lau Tzu in various versions,
And spent whole summers reading the Psalms.
I've harked to Beethoven, Bach, and Brahms,
And braved cosmogony led by Jeans,
Attempting by such exacting means
To richen my mind. With what result?
I find it is still more difficult
To keep my treasure. Though here and there
Cling random granules, my mind stays bare,
Quite unimproved by the help I give.
There's just no way to improve a sieve!

Philosophy Is What You Make It

PHILOSOPHY IS WHAT YOU MAKE IT

When life is rough and skies are gray,
My comment is a terse one:
Tomorrow is another day . . .
Quite probably a worse one!

LINES COMPOSED IN A CORNER

My objection to secret vices
Is not that people indulge 'em,
But that this rarely suffices:
They're dithering to divulge 'em!

WILLY-NILLY, BACILLI

Man stoutly labors with science and heart and soul,
Trying to keep bacilli under control.
Each sturdy bacillus musters the strength of ten
And doggedly tries to do the same with men.

UTOPIA UNLIMITED

When we achieve an ideal state,
Every woman will have a mate,
While men, when this glad day occurs,
Will all be footloose bachelors.

HISTORICAL FOOT-NOTE

To reach Fame's eminence sublime
So hard a road the hero marches
That footprints on the sands of time
Are often marked with fallen arches.

WORM'S-EYE VIEW OF A CLASSIC THEME

Whatever the troubles of poor little rich girls,
Whatever woes they may suffer,
I'm still convinced that poor little poor girls
Have it a whole lot tougher!

SEEING THE BRIGHT SIDE

Though clobbered by trouble, grief, and woe,
I cling to the philosophical theme:
Someday I'll look back on this, I know,
And laugh till my straitjacket splits a seam!

OH, MY ACHING VOID!

The fact that I can't take it with me
Is something I do not mind.
What grieves me is this:
It appears that I'll miss
The chance to leave any behind!

BLESS MY LITTLE HEART

Oh, what a good girl am I!
And here is the why and wherefore:
I never am tempted by
Temptations I do not care for.

THE TROUBLE WITH GENERALIZATIONS

Although they are flowers of wisdom,
No sooner do we propound them
Than myriad stout exceptions
Spring up like weeds around them.

SONG UNDER A LEAKY APHORISM

The rain falls from unbiased skies
On rich and poor, the sages tell us . . .
But rarely mention money buys
Some very water-proof umbrellas.

REGRETTABLE TIMING

Alas, when God devised His plan,
He hadn't yet created man,
And missed the fine advice the latter
Could have provided in the matter.

WISE QUACK

How little availed my truckling
To the fickle goddess Luck.
For I was an ugly duckling,
And now I'm an ugly duck!

SO SORRY!

An apology is the double play
Of firing a parting shot
By saying you're sorry in such a way
It's perfectly clear you're not.

IN DEFENSE OF THE HIGHBROW

Believe me, it isn't a pose he strikes
To impress us hoi polloi.
A highbrow's a person who really likes
The things he doesn't enjoy.

LET SLEEPING STATISTICS LIE

Statistics show that many more people die
In bed than elsewhere, establishing thereby
A fact statistic-lovers can have no doubt of:
Beds are places the prudent will stay out of.

PREPONDERANT INGREDIENT

When social eminence is discussed,
    I'm heard to mutter low:
Today what it takes to be Upper Crust
    Is mainly dough.

INTROVERT'S LAMENT

Within my solitude I long
To be a part of some gay throng
Whose revels, unrestrained and rude,
Would make me long for solitude.

DOUBLE-EDGED SAW

The early bird will catch the worm,
Or so the proverb likes to state.
The moral: wise birds rise betimes,
But even wiser worms sleep late.

WHO AM I TO CONDEMN

Everyone makes mistakes,
And judging them isn't my line.
I'm tolerant to a fault . . .
Especially if it's mine.

PAY-OFF

Reviewing those errors I'll own as such,
I'll say of my worst offenses:
It's not my mistakes I regret so much
As their troublesome consequences.

ONE PER EACH

For every dog there is a flea,
For every rose, a nettle.
For every bonnet there's a bee;
A pot for every kettle.

And in her wisdom, Fate will send
A goose for every gander;
For every human fault a friend
To point it out with candor!

FUNDAMENTAL FALLACY

Utopia still will be far to seek
As ever it's been, so long
As men believe they can strengthen the weak
By weakening the strong.

ON THE HIGH COST OF PRIMROSES

Middle-age's chief defense
Against temptation isn't sense:
It's the expense!

REVERIE ON WILSHIRE BLVD.

I never see a lady pass
In diamonds and mink,
A member of the Moneyed Class,
But what I stop and think:

"Now, there but by the grace of God
Go I." And then I shrug,
Repeat it, very sagely nod,
And kick a fireplug.

The Man in the Aisle Seat

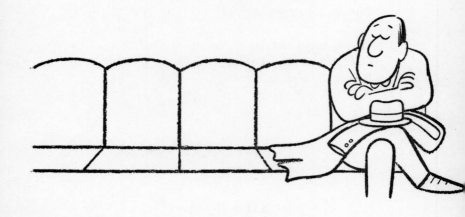

THE MAN IN THE AISLE SEAT

I'm always early, I'm never late.
I'm in my seat on the aisle by eight,
So that all of the people who arrive
At eight-oh-two or eight-oh-five
Or eight-fifteen will have to squeeze
And wriggle around my stubborn knees,
On which quite frequently I have put
My overcoat, while an outstretched foot
Is held in reserve, with mutters and grunts,
For dealing with any later dunce.

And if anyone in my row is seated
Ahead of me, he needn't feel cheated:
In the ancient theatrical tradition,
I'll fix him good at the intermission!

THE SECRET LIFE OF MRS. MITTY

She peels potatoes, dreaming the scene:
She's star-eyed, lush, and glamorous,
A silken queen of the silver screen,
With a hero dark and amorous,
Who draws her to him, intense and yearning . . .
When oh my heavens, the roast is burning!

The duke is a rich and regal laird,
But she, his adorable duchess,
Blazing with priceless gems, is snared
In a handsome villain's clutches:
Blackmail! . . . letters! . . . What course to choose? . . .
When the washer decides to blow a fuse.

A fabulous international spy,
And never seductress braver,
She hears her sentence: condemned to die!
But her lover will surely save her.
They'll flee to Paris or maybe Rome . . .
But not at the moment: Walter's home.

ON A CERTAIN SPINSTER

One blenches to think how the Lord was chided
In terse and vinegar accents when
She learned that for women He had provided
Nothing better to marry than *men!*

THE ENCHANTRESS

He sits like a nice well-mannered dog,
While around him his good wife's monologue
Flows as the river of time through space,
A tender expression on his face.

And now and again, he nods and smiles,
"Yes, dear . . . yes, darling . . ." which trick beguiles
The lady to further colloquy.
So she is happy, and so is he.

For he never hints and she never guesses
What dream of women he fondly Yesses.

A REAL COMFORT

Whenever my world's shot full of holes
And wormwood slosheth my cup,
I know I can count on Tessie Boles
To rally and cheer me up.

For never the cloud, in Tessie's book,
But is lined with solid sterling.
And things are rarely as bad as they look,
And a bright new day's unfurling.

We all have troubles, dear Tess avers,
And mine, if I face the facts,
Are probably no whit worse than hers,
So why don't I just relax?

For Tessie's one of those optimists
Who spits in the eye of woe,
And with glowing cheerfulness, she insists
That I follow suit, and so

That's why I'm devoted to Merton Groat,
Who, when my life gets tough,
Sighs dolefully and remarks (I quote),
"Jeepers, you're having it *rough!*"

ANTHROPOMORPHOUS REX

Oh, gone is the day of royal apotheosis,
When Majesties were verily majestic,
Their nourishment ingested by osmosis,
Their lives Olympian, not dull domestic.
Their loyal subjects now may consume with relish
Detailed reports that intimately illumine
Those sovereign flaws and foibles that embellish
Rex and Regina, proven all too human.

Happy the minion of the queen with glasses,
The king whose heartburn stabs him *in excelsis.*
Such imperfections cheer the Middle Classes.
If Royalty's much like anybody else is,
The rule, inverted, certainly must be
That anybody is much like Royalty.

CROSS-FIRE

She gives me the dirt on you. Then she
Regales you with shocking tales of me,
As busily back and forth she wends,
Burning her scandal at both ends.

ON A TOO-BOUNTIFUL LADY

Whoever begs a shilling
Shall have at least a pound.
Who asks a cup of water
In wine is nearly drowned.

Whose need is simple friendship
With ardent love must cope.
Whoever takes her bounty
Is mortgaged past all hope!

MACHINE-AGE THRENODY

Oh, I'm the sort of person machinery hates.
For me the wily household appliance waits,
Wires crossed and gear-teeth bared in a fiendish grin,
Just daring me to go on and plug it in.

For me the mangle mangles the clothes it mangles;
The sweeper gobbles its cord in tattered tangles.
It's I who keep the sewing machine in stitches.
Just let me flick the diabolical switches
Of waxer or mixer, and heaven protect the fuses!
At my approach, whatever's mechanical loses
Its sense of subservience and plays the master,
Be it zipper, potato peeler, or simple castor.

I'm the only person I know who's endured the trial
Of getting her finger stuck in a telephone dial.
Machinery hates me. And I'm past concealing
The fact that this is a warmly mutual feeling!

LADIES MEETING

What makes you think
They're not sincere?
Their screams of, *"Darling!"*
Echo clear
As, matching mink,
A gushing pair,
They touch cool cheeks
And kiss the air.

NARROW ESCAPE

Rather than be alone,
He'll make a boon companion
Of someone quite unknown,
So solitude's dark canyon
Can't yawn its awful gulf
And plunge him to the danger
Of being by himself,
An even stranger stranger.

THE MONOLOGUE

His tireless monologue plods on and on.
And I can picture, straining back a yawn,
A caravan of words that seems to wind
Across vast windy deserts of the mind
Where no green thought abates the desolation.
And he, mistaking glass-eyed desperation
For rapt attention, happily expands
And sends more nomads out across the sands.

IRRITANT INCARNATE

He isn't malicious, he isn't evil,
But if life were oatmeal, he'd be a weevil.
If life were a shoe, he'd be a tack in it.
If life were a mirror, he'd be a crack in it.

He isn't a brute, a rogue, nor a villain,
But if life were a molar in need of a fillin',
This innocent soul, so free of depravity,
Would be a berry seed lodged in the cavity!

CORNELIA

Oh, time cannot quench nor comparison smother
The fires of Cornelia, the Absolute Mother,
That doting dispenser of vitamins, gruels,
And monologues brilliant with tales of her jewels.
Let dictators topple and scamper like weasels:
Cornelia regales you with Johnny Boy's measles.
Let earthquakes run rampant from Nome to Peoria:
Hark to how Sister won't take her Castoria.

Hark to their drolleries, cutely refulgent;
To marvelous mischief, of which she's indulgent.
Give ear and conclude that her juvenile menaces
Must be the outcome of parthenogenesis.
Verily, who could infer that a pater
Co-authored these gems, when Cornelia's their mater?—
The mother of angels, her reverent litany
Hints that no man in the world could begitany!

EPITAPH ON A COQUETTE

Immaculate at last and free
Of earthly lust and vanity,
  That loveliest of souls.
But, lifelong habit holding sway,
No doubt the sweet compliant clay
  Is flirting with the moles.

LOW-COST HOLOCAUST

Aroused, his ire
Is a raging fire
  That nothing can snuff
  Or palliate,
But which, be it marked,
Is never sparked
  By anyone tough
  And big enough
  To call his bluff
  And retaliate!

PARADOX

Now here is a paradox, none absurder:
The nicest people sometimes do murder,
While many stinkers lead blameless lives,
Piously faithful to badgered wives.
They wear clean shirts, but their thoughts are dingy.
They do their duty, but oh, they're stingy.
They're not caught gambling, cheating, nor stealing,
But they could teach Shylock some tricks in dealing.
They stay out of jails, they stay out of breadlines.
But now and again they make the headlines,
Cast as the victims of quite a few
Of the murders the nicest people do.

ADESTE FIDELES

The anthem thunders to its close,
And as the echo dwindles off
We hear the muted bark of those
Who came to pray, remained to cough.

The rector's sermon now begins:
He skips the tattered Seven Sins
And concentrates on Inward Peace.
Ah, blessèd season of release
When, lifted by his earnest gust,
Our spirits rise and float like dust
In stained-glass realms of light above:
Salvation . . . God . . . Eternal Love . . .
Where some remain aloft in glory
Till halfway through the offertory.

Then out into the noonday sun
Where life is pressing and untidy,
Where Sunday roasts are overdone
And Ladies' Guild will meet on Friday.

DEATH OF THE SOLIPSIST

Today they interred the Solipsist,
That old philosopher who believed
Creation didn't and couldn't exist
Except as his consciousness conceived.

People engendered by his thought
Stood by his grave and saw him laid
Into the earth his dream had wrought,
While a conceptual parson prayed.

They lowered him into the fictive loam,
Figments bowed by a kindly sorrow.
They buried his cosmos and went home
Still certain the sun would rise tomorrow.

The Facts of Love

THE FACTS OF LOVE

By now I have learned the facts of love.
I know what the passion's fashioned of.
I've danced to the piper and met his terms.
I've bitten the apple and met the worms.
And love, I say, is a dew-pearled rose
With a bee sequestered to sting your nose.
It's milk and honey laced with gall,
And a roller skate in a darkened hall.

It's the mill over which I've thrown my bonnet
To paradise with a mortgage on it.
It's a beckoning rainbow with a pot
Of trouble at the end, that's what.
And knowing of love what I know about it,
Why, oh why can't I live without it!

THESE ENDURING YOUNG CHARMS

Such beauty as may brave my flaws
Admire, beloved. Enjoy it,
But never let it be a cause
For love. Time will destroy it.

And love me not for wit, my lord.
For though it please you Sunday,
Remember wit's a fickle sword,
And it may pierce you Monday.

Nor more my virtues, dear, exalt;
They tend to waver badly.
But love me for each sturdy fault,
And you'll love long and madly!

MY OWN TRUE LOVE

There's nobody sweet as my true love is;
Nobody's smile as merry as his.
And if there are others who feel the same . . .
Well, as he says, he isn't to blame.

Oh, nobody's dear as my own true love.
Who else could pledge me the moon above
With vows so beautiful when he makes them
I even believe them when he breaks them.

For he is my love come foul or fair.
There's nobody like him anywhere.
I worship the ground his light feet tread,
With stars in my eyes and rocks in my head!

PRELUDE TO AN INSURRECTION

We should be one, believes my love:—
One heart, one mind, one neat set of
Convictions and opinions, viz,
His!

STILL ME WITH CARESSES

This way you have to silence me is pleasant,
A trick that keeps me tractable and meek.
When I would talk I find my lips quiescent
Beneath your kiss, and so I do not speak.

By all means, lover, still me with caresses.
Pour kisses on my mouth like wine to drink,
And drown the rush of syllables and phrases . . .
Lest I should tell you what I really think.

MODERN DIAGNOSIS

Dido, Sappho, and Elaine
Wept and ached and smarted.
And to the world their plight was plain:
They were broken-hearted.

Dido, Sappho, and Elaine
Were lovely and exotic.
And wailing with the selfsame pain,
What am I? Neurotic!

LOVE WILL DISTRACT ME NO MORE

Though love is done, I'm glad to say
I do not mope, my dear.
I go about my tasks each day
And rarely shed a tear.

I hang the kittens on their pegs,
And comb the morning mail,
And sew the buttons on the eggs,
And dust the ginger ale.

I rake and water down the rug,
And then I take a walk,
And if I meet a fireplug,
I stand a while and talk.

Oh, I am busy all day through,
For which I'm very glad.
For otherwise I'd think of you,
My darling, and go mad.

LOW COMEDY

I might maintain some dignity
If love, in taking leave of me,
Should try to knife me in the side,
Or dose my tea with cyanide,
Or strangle me up some dark alley,
To show we'd reached the grand finale.

Such gestures speak of high romance
And tragedy. But what's my chance
Of keeping pride and poise intact
When love concludes our little act
By taking aim and letting fly
A well-directed custard pie!

ARS GRATIA GROCER

Out of the ashes of my passion,
Mixed with sweat and tears, I fashion
My poignant songs. Love's dead, I know,
But I'm alive, and that takes dough.

STRAW IN AN ILL WIND

I'm wrong, you're right: that's that, you say;
No further words we'll squander.
My love, against a bitter day,
Here's something you might ponder:

Your headlong arrogance is such
I long to kick or strike you,
For though I love you very much,
It's getting hard to like you!

GODMOTHER'S SONG

You shall have moonlight,
But never the moon.
You shall have honey,
But never the bee.
You shall have birdsong
By night and by noon,
But never the songbird
That sings in the tree.
Oh, you shall have moonlight
And love, late or soon,
But never the lover
And never the moon.

THORNS ON THE ROSE TREE

Would you have solitude?
Then you must be lonely.
Is it love you cry for?
Learn how to bear
Daily propinquity,
Cares pressing stonily.
Life makes the bargain.
Of course it isn't fair.

Thorns on the rose tree,
Tears behind the laughter,
Bills in the mailbox . . .
Life has a rule:
Take what you want of it;
Pay the tab thereafter.
Can you evade it?
Don't be a fool!

BIRD WATCHER'S SONG

Her hair is from the raven,
Her breast is from the dove,
And from a linnet came the voice
Of my love's other love.

Her grace is from the swallow,
My rival's. And it's plain
Some nameless little feathered friend
Contributed her brain.

MY ONE AND ONLY

Oh, my love's not a man you would pick from a crowd,
But whatever shortcomings afflict him
　　Look charmingly small
　　When I stop to recall
It was not from a crowd that I picked him!

ROUNDEL ON AN APPROPRIATE SUBJECT

This too shall pass . . . as dewdrops on the sward,
As shattered roses sifting on the grass.
This pot-pourri of penance and reward,
This too shall pass.

The tempers clashing, angry brass on brass,
The hopes doubt crushed and faith has not restored,
Shall fade as ciphers from a frosty glass.

Then shall our hearts find peace in sweet accord.
We'll kiss and turn away and sigh, "Alas!"
For love affairs must end, and thank the Lord
This too shall pass!

SMALL HINT
TO A BIG WHEEL

Sweet sir, the fellows who snare
My female heart every time
Don't tell me how wonderful they're;
They tell me how wonderful I'm.

OLD, OLD DREAM

Now, my love, that your wounds are kissed,
Your doubts allayed and your sins dismissed,
Your troubles made pygmy by my charms,
I cradle you soft within my arms
And stroke your brow and quietly weave
A dream that must have begun with Eve:—

That someday a man will come along,
A man reliable, kind, and strong,
Who'll take me to his generous breast
And hear my sorrows and fears confessed,
And smooth my hair and forgive my crimes,
And allow me to be the child sometimes.

BALLADE OF THE DEPENDABLE ESCORT

At parties, I almost always meet
Attractive fellows who give me the eye:
Say, one of the spiritual Elite,
With spirits low as his brow is high.
And off in a corner he tells me why.
Yes, in half an hour he has quite unstrung me
With tales of his Freudian wish to die.
So I'll go home with the guy what brung me.

Or chance it I'm toppled off my feet
By a man of distinction, suave and shy,
Who whispers presently, most discreet,
That he's bound by a matrimonial tie
To a lady who doesn't even try
To understand him. Oh, this one's sung me
His threnody till my eyes were dry.
So I'll go home with the guy what brung me.

Or now and again Fate gives me a treat
And offers a downright sweetie-pie
Who doubles my pulse's normal beat
As I beam at this maiden's dream and sigh,
"At last! An ointment without a fly!"
But look at the rest of the deal Fate's flung me:
His plighted blonde stands watchfully by.
So I'll go home with the guy what brung me.

L'Envoi
Prince, it were pointless to deny
That your lack of glamour has often stung me.
But better men are in short supply,
So I'll go home with the guy what brung me!

VALENTINE FOR YEAR-ROUND USE

Now, tell me why a rooster crows,
And why an onion's not a rose,
And why a salmon swims upstream,
And why a maiden needs her dream.
And tell me why a cat likes nip,
And why a well-adjusted hip-
Popotamus will lavish kisses
On his hippopotamrs.
And I'll tell you, my darling, why
The moon's suspended in the sky,
And glowworms glow and pigeons coo
And I love you.

A Seizure of Couplets

A SEIZURE OF COUPLETS
Fit the First

The prophet is without honor till the year
He prophesies the things we want to hear.

The flaws in greatness don't one tittle
Increase the stature of the little.

The trust of dogs and children proves this rule:
Dogs and children are not hard to fool.

That Caesar and his slave within their graves
Are equal is no balm to living slaves.

Their iron chains struck off, behold
Men fight to put on chains of gold.

He who fights and runs away
May be a general some day.

What sight doth so infuriate the wise
As seeing fools happy in their paradise?

It is the pedant, not the peasant,
Who makes the poet's life unpleasant.

Only the dry wood may be kindled;
Only the greedy may be swindled.

Diplomacy is pretending not to note
In others a strong desire to slit your throat.

A neutral is a man who ends
With two new foes and two less friends.

Get thee behind me, Satan, and be quick.
Methinks a little push might turn the trick.

Reform the Devil: he'll profess
To teach the angels holiness.

After the seven sins, the Devil wrought
An eighth and deadlier sin called Getting Caught.

So long as money is evil's root,
The tree will bear attractive fruit.

Vowing our faith in heaven, still we go
Like exiles driven from the hell we know.

In the city of the mad, the sane
Are held in check with bar and chain.

What man would be his brother's keeper
When sanitariums are cheaper?

Your broken leg will never rend
My heart as does my hangnail, friend.

Psychosomatic illnesses are those
The doctor cannot promptly diagnose.

Oh, how the angels must have enjoyed
The meeting between St. Paul and St. Freud!

Alas, no revelation from above
Makes clear which church God is a member of.

Fit the Second

It's true that man invented cloth
But Nature topped him with the moth.

How many a genius was just a crackpot
Until he managed to hit the jackpot.

Nothing is offered in more abundance
By TV announcers than redundance!

Absence makes the heart grow fonder . . .
Of whom let absent lovers ponder.

The apple Adam ate to Eden's loss
Was probably served up as apple sauce.

By using intuition a woman can
Guess right about as often as a man.

The follies of youth become, O sage,
The vaunted experience of age.

Blood's thicker than water, but then that's true
Of sarsaparilla, ink, and glue.

While some to the purple are born and bred,
Most of us spend our lives in the red.

Were wealth the burden the rich declare it,
Be sure they'd compel the poor to share it.

To see myself as others see me
Would make me swear it couldn't be me!

Success is a test where it may be said:
The smaller the man, the bigger the head.

Politicians' well-ground axes
Don't get dull from cutting taxes.

An appointive office is that which is held by someone
Who helped an elective officer to become one.

I live as ungraciously as I'm able:
I cook on a stove and eat at a table.

When a woman looks wistful and tender and pensive,
She's probably thinking of something expensive.

That God made time the stars attest,
But clocks were Satan's little jest.

A paradoxical chase is this we stage,
Who hotly pursue long life as we dodge old age.

The little white lie is the balm that soothes
The hornet stabs of little black truths.

Ten Mother Hubbards on a nude
Won't make a prude one whit less lewd.

When *I* was your age, O benighted youth,
I was just as benighted as you, forsooth.

How very self-centered people can be!
They think of themselves instead of me.

A diamond, it should be understood,
Is just a piece of carbon that made good.

Two things in life I've had and ample:
Good advice and bad example.

Summary

SUMMARY

What have I learned since I was twenty?
Colloquially speaking, plenty!
I've learned I'm neither worse nor better,
My sins no blacker, tears no wetter
Than average. Within my store
Of learning lurk these bits of lore:
There never was an idle rumor;
The most important sense is humor;
And poverty is no disgrace
Except within the human race.
I've learned that cowardice will claim
Patience for its other name;
And jealousy's a symptom of
The manic ego, not of love.

I've also learned that men are far
More prudish than their ladies are;
That trusting either sex is risky;
That fiction, flattery, and whisky
Should be imbibed in moderation;
And I have learned to look temptation
Straight in the eye and count the cost
And yield without a moment lost.
I've learned the virtue of a lie;
Which fork to use for humble pie;
The ashen taste of vain regret,
And much I wish I could forget!

AU 'VOIR

When the love is old,
And the sweet is bitter,
And the hearth is cold,
And no birds twitter
At dusk and dawn
In the circling boughs,
It is time to be gone
From the past's bleak house.

So the door is shut,
And I firmly lock it.
I am going . . . *but*
With the key in my pocket.

MAJOR WOE OF A MINOR POET

Down the corridors of time
Echoes silver-sad the rhyme
Of other star-crossed bards who bore
Ills as dire with hearts as sore.

Fate a jade and fame a bubble;
Fickle love and constant trouble:
Epic theme and lyric grist,
Poets long have sung the list
Of woes like mine. And what is worse,
They did it in much better verse!

OVER-DUE TRIBUTE

Ah, when I'm beat and bent with care,
Who seats me in a cosy chair
And weeps for every bruise and crack
I take, and pats me on the back?
Who chortles at my mildest jest,
And vows that I deserve the best? . . .
Has done so since I was a tot,
And will when I am old, God wot?

Who labors for me like a slave,
And knows I'm good and kind and brave
And free of malice as a lamb?
Who loves me just the way I am,
And is beyond the slightest doubt
The person I can't live without,
To think on whom my heart nigh melts?
Me! Who else?

AT A CONCERT OF AVANT-GARDE JAZZ

Was it for this that, back in time,
We wriggled gamely from the slime;
Developed brains, however small;
Became the stout Neanderthal;
Contrived the wheel and captured fire;
Built Ur and Nineveh and Tyre?
Was it for this that Sappho plained,
That Socrates in sorrow drained
The hemlock till his wisdom slept?
For this that gentle Jesus wept,
Aquinas prayed, da Vinci wrought,
Chopin composed and Einstein thought? . . .

That men who neither thirst nor lack
For riboflavin, Univac,
And aspirin should now thus ravage
The cosmic harmony with savage
Unmeaning din, and I should sit
Pretending I'm enjoying it?
For this we dreamed and fought and bled?
If so, we shoulda stood in bed!

PROPOSED AMENDMENT

Just now I'm sunk in misery
So deep the one escape I see
Is via death. For while the morrow
May shine triumphant over sorrow,
Today's so steeped in grief that I
Would give most anything to die.
At least I would give anything
But life . . . and there's the serpent's sting.
For every way I'd be content
With death, except it's permanent.
Could I but alter Nature's laws,
I'd add a codicil or clause
Which mercifully would provide
For temporary suicide!

MY FACE IS MY MISFORTUNE

I have a face that people trust.
They all too evidently must,
Since into its now-calloused ears
They pour the sagas of their years,
Their secret sins and woes and ills
And love affairs and dental bills,
Until I'd trade my pan for one
That looked as if I packed a gun,
Or pilfered from a blind man's cup,
Or anyway, would just get up
And walk away, instead of listen
As I am doomed to do with this'n!

BE GOOD, SWEET MAID

Be good, sweet maid. Leave sin to seasoned sinners
Who've learned the art of temperance in vice;
Who of forbidden fruit do not make dinners,
But use it merely as a nibbled spice.

The simple virtuous who take one swallow
Equate whole orchards with a single seed,
And feeling hellfire sealed and sure to follow,
Cast off restraint and gorge with hopeless greed.

Successful rogues are disciplined gourmets
With senses both of humor and proportion,
And one who takes the tempting morsel pays
The going rate, my child, but not extortion.

Such civil knaves would scorn to sup beside you.
They sin, sweet maid, like gentlemen and ladies,
While you, unless you let your conscience guide you,
Would find it rode you headlong into Hades.

O LOVELY SINS

O lovely sins, I must repent:
Your sweets with guilt must leaven,
Ruing your pleasures, penitent,
So I can go to heaven . . .
Where, being paradise, it's plain
No bliss shall be forbidden,
And I can sin you all again,
Unblushing and unchidden.

I TOO AM ON THE SIDE
OF THE ANGELS

Wherefore I don't disparage
Simians, since it's clear
That angels, being angels,
Can move among us here
Corporeally accoutred
In any guise or shape,
And how can I be certain
An angel's not an ape?

NEW YEAR'S GREETING TO MY
FAVORITE PLANET

So, little earth, again we've done
Our giddy loop around the sun.
In spite of isms, cataclysms,
Schisms, heaves, and rheumatisms,
Assorted lightning bolts and nuts,
We've kept our orbits . . . or our ruts.
You've had earthquakes; I, l'amour,
For which, per each, there is no cure.
You've had floods and ice and fire;
I've had tears, advice, and ire.
You've had satellites and rockets;
I've had holes in all my pockets.

Yes, winter, spring . . . now, there's a season!
You know that spring could be the reason
We don't just quit? . . . that spring of ours! . . .
With summer rising from the flowers,
Then autumn, tawny under haze,
And winter . . . all those lovely days
Our troubles render no less sweet.
So come on, earth! Get on your feet!
We've got a future to explore.
Let's go round the sun once more!